Essential Jazz Lines

in the style of wes montgomery

by corey christiansen

This book of original musical studies and analyses by Corey Christiansen is designed to help you develop your own personal improvising style.

Online Audio   www.melbay.com/99905BCDEB

D1477766

AUDIO CONTENTS

2 3 4 5 6 7 8 9 0

Visit us on the Web at www.melbay.com — E-mail us at email@melbay.com

Table of Contents

Wes Montgomery Introduction

Wes Montgomery took jazz guitar to a new level when he came to the public's attention in the late 1950's. Known for his fluid lines and his big jazz guitar sound, Wes influenced thousands of guitarists in the styles of jazz, blues, and rock.

Using the thumb of his right hand and playing a Gibson L-5, Wes created a sound that guitarists have envied for decades. Wes secured his seat in the congregation of jazz greats by relying on incredible ears, great understanding of the fretboard, excellent technique, fantastic time, and musical knowledge of the jazz giants that came before him. Lionel Hampton first hired him because he could play the solos of Charlie Christian note for note. He learned the style of Charlie Christian and Charlie Parker and then combined their material with is own to create his timeless, unique style.

This book will present some of the soloing techniques that Wes used as well has present many melodic ideas (lines) similar to the way he played over the chord progressions in many jazz standards. Because the major and minor ii-V-I progression are the most widely used chord progressions in jazz standards, the lines in this text will work over these progressions. The accompanying audio contains many play-along tracks (vamps of one chord and vamps around the circle of fourths) that the student should use to practice the material in one key and then master it in all twelve keys.

By learning the techniques used by Wes Montgomery, guitarists will add to their own improvising arsenal. As improvising musicians add to their collection of musical ideas, their ability to express themselves completely increases. Have fun studying these ideas and applying them in improvised solos.

Wes Montgomery and Charlie Parker

The following chapters on Guide Tones, Bebop Scales, 3 to ♭9, Playing the Upper-Structure/Secondary Arpeggios, Targeting, Arpeggios, Playing Octaves, Block Chords, Chord Substitutions and Solo Development will help students understand the music of Wes Montgomery and see how his music was inspired by Charlie Parker. (Chapters on Guide Tones, Bebop Scales, 3 to ♭9, Playing the Upper-Structure/Secondary Arpeggios and Targeting are also found in "Essential Jazz Lines—In the Style of Charlie Parker.") These chapters will also shed light on the techniques Wes pioneered on guitar and make it easier for students to understand the music played by Wes Montgomery.

Guide Tones

Guide tones are the notes in a chord which lead or give harmonic pull toward the next chord. A simple ii-V-I progression will demonstrate how guide tones work. In the ii-V progression, notice that the seventh degree in the Dm7 chord (C) leads to the third of the G7 chord (B) by a half step. The same can be seen in a V-I progression. The seventh of G7 (F) leads to the third of C7 (E) by half step.

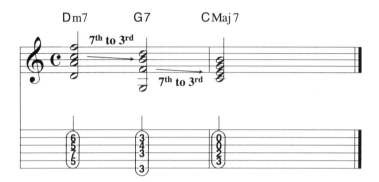

The example below shows how one might use guide tones. By utilizing guide tones, a soloist is able to enhance the harmonic "pull" generated by the ii-V-I progression.

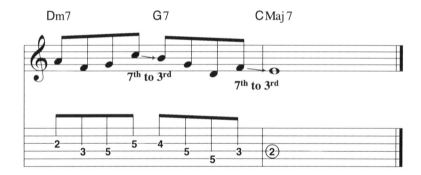

Bebop Scales

There are three basic bebop scales. The Mixolydian (dominant seventh) bebop scale can be used primarily against dominant seventh chords. The Dorian bebop scale is used primarily against minor seventh chords. The major bebop scale is used primarily against major sixth and major seventh chords. Each of these scales is an eight-note scale rather than the typical seven-note scale.

The Mixolydian bebop scale differs from the Mixolydian mode in that it has an extra note between the root and the flatted seventh degree of the regular Mixolydian mode. This Mixolydian bebop scale is shown below.

Mixolydian Bebop
(played against dominant seventh chords)

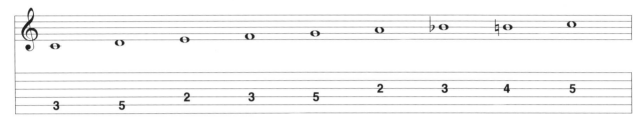

Mixolydian Bebop

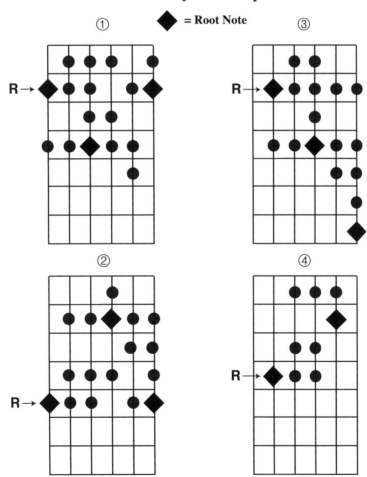

* The scale diagram and fingerings in this book are only suggestions. Each student should experiment with their own fingerings.

When a musician starts on a chord tone and plays this scale with eighth notes, each of the chord tones in a dominant seventh scale will be played on downbeats (strong beats). Because the bebop scales are eight-note scales, it takes exactly four counts to play each scale using eighth notes.

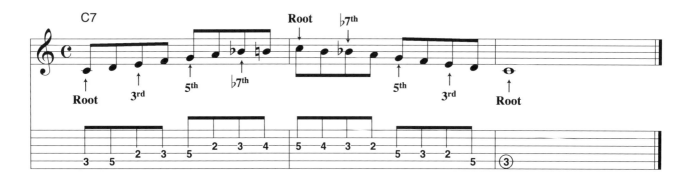

The following musical example shows how one might use this scale when soloing over a dominant seventh chord.

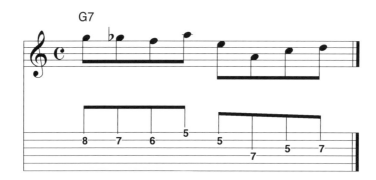

The Dorian bebop scale differs from the Dorian mode in that it has an extra note between the flatted third and fourth intervals of the regular Dorian mode. The Dorian bebop scale is shown below.

Dorian Bebop
(played against minor seventh chords)

Dorian Bebop

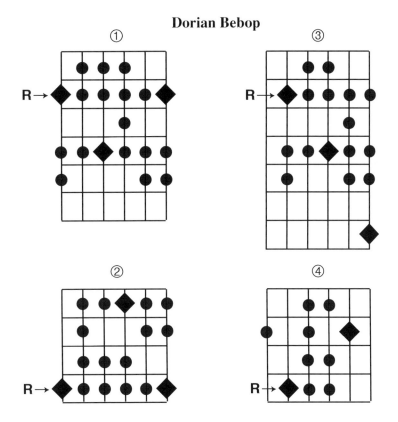

The Dorian bebop scale is an eight-note scale and will take exactly four beats to play if eighth notes are employed. However, not all of the chord tones of the respective minor seventh chord will be played on downbeats if one starts on a chord tone. Many jazz musicians utilize this scale by starting on the fourth of the chord (a G note when playing against a Dm7) and leading to the third (F) chromatically. An example of how one would use this technique is shown below. Sometimes jazz musicians treat minor seventh chords as a dominant seventh chord a fourth away. This means they can play G7 material against Dm7 chords.

D Dorian Bebop or G Mixolydian Bebop

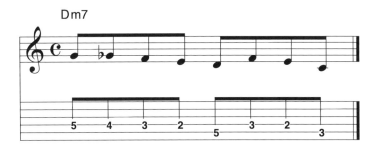

The major bebop scale differs from the major scale in that it has an extra note between the fifth and sixth degrees of the regular major scale. The major bebop scale is shown below.

Major Bebop

(played against major seventh chords)

Major Bebop

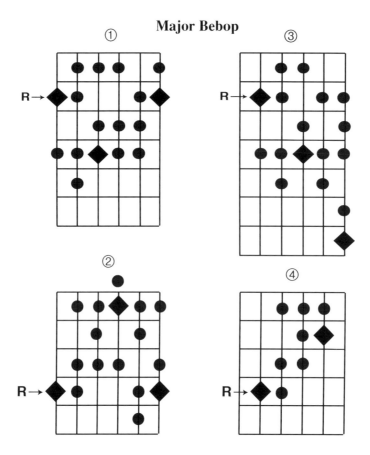

Like the other bebop scales, the major bebop scale is an eight-note scale and will take exactly four beats to play if eighth notes are used. If one starts on a chord tone and plays this scale utilizing eighth notes, each of the chord tones in the respective major sixth chord will be played on downbeats. An example of how one might use this scale to improvise is shown below.

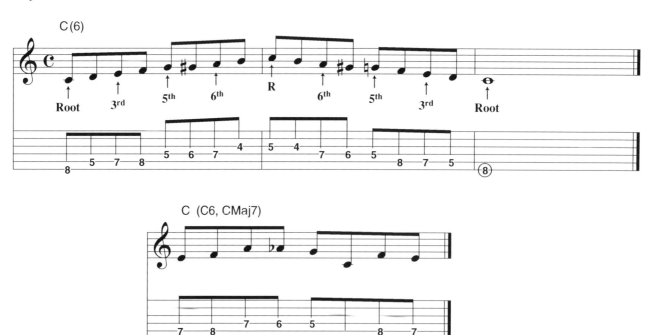

3 to ♭9

Three to flat nine is a technique that Charlie Parker pioneered and used over dominant seventh chords. Most great jazz soloists are aware of this sound and have used it at one time or another. If the chord being played is a G7, the third is B and the flat nine is an A flat. There are a number of ways to get from the third to the flat nine. The first and most obvious way is by skip. Move from the third and ascend to the flat nine or move from the third and descend to the flat nine. Examples of this are shown below.

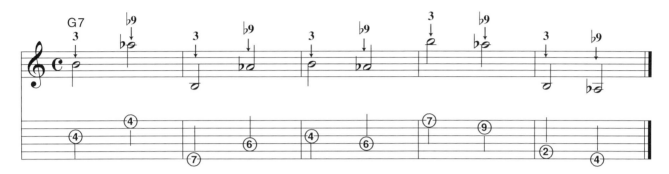

Another way to get from the third to the flat nine is by way of a diminished arpeggio. A diminished seventh arpeggio consists of nothing but minor third intervals. To build a diminished seventh arpeggio from a G7 chord, start with the third of the G7 (B), and then play a D (moving up or down). Next, ascend or descend to the minor seventh of the chord (F). From the F, ascend or descend to an A flat. The direction of the arpeggio doesn't have to start and continue in only one direction. In fact, it sounds interesting when the direction changes.

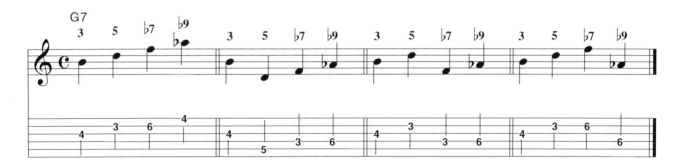

The third to flat nine sounds good when a dominant seventh chord resolves to a major chord a fourth away (G7-Cmajor). In the case of G7 to C, the flat nine (A♭) leads to a G note, which is the fifth of a C, major chord.

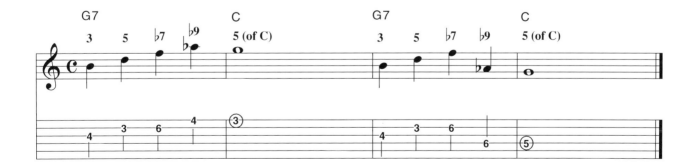

The lines found below show how one might use this technique in a V-I chord progression.

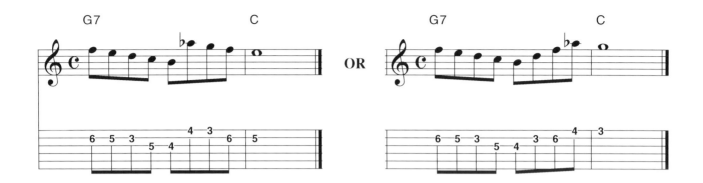

It is important to practice these techniques in all twelve keys. With practice, this material will flow effortlessly while improvising.

Below are chord diagrams showing a few fingerings for third to flat nine movements on guitar. Remember that skips and arpeggios may be used in any direction.

3 to ♭9
Fingering Charts

(R) = Root Note

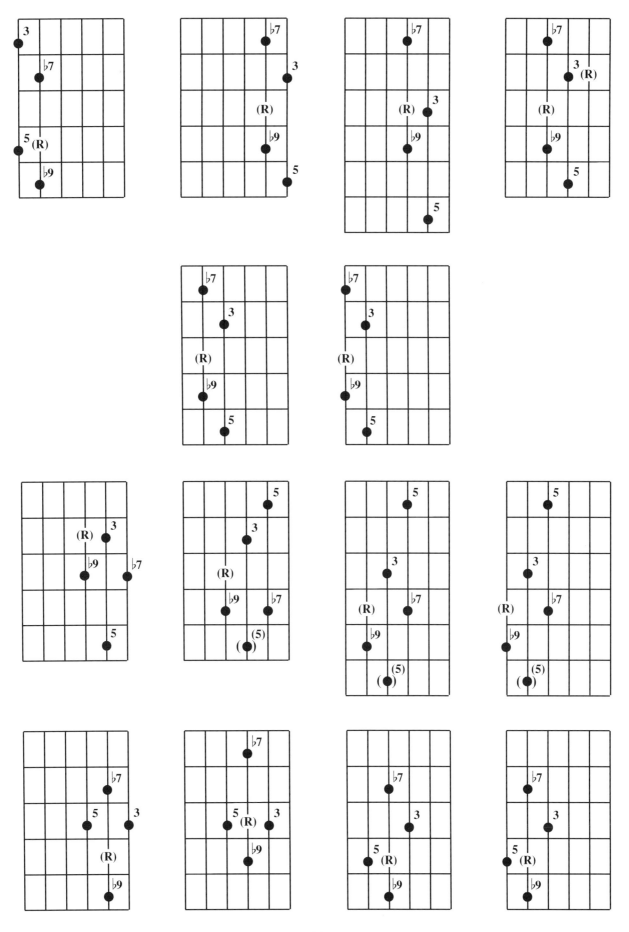

Playing the Upper-Structure of Chords

(Secondary Arpeggios)

The upper-structure of a chord is any note in the chord above the seventh. For example, a Cmaj7 chord consists of a root (C), major third (E), perfect fifth (G), and major seventh (B). These notes are derived from the C major scale. The upper-structure chord-tones (extensions) of the Cmaj7 chord are the ninth (D), eleventh (F), and the thirteenth (A). The way in which these notes relate to the major scale is shown below.

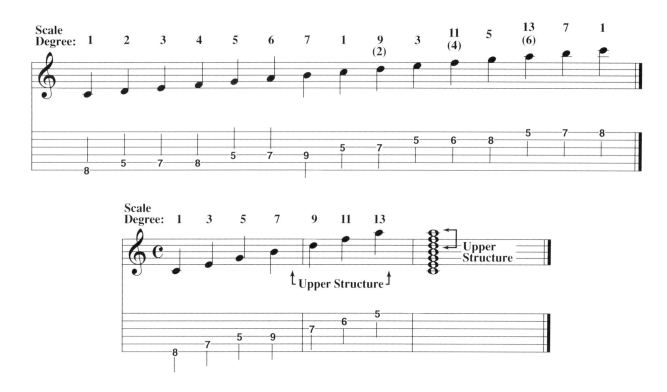

To begin using this technique, start on the third of any chord (major, minor or dominant seventh) and arpeggiate up to the ninth. An example of how this technique would be used against a D minor seventh chord is shown below.

Dm7

Notice the notes from this example are the same notes contained in an Fmaj7 chord. Standing by itself, the upper-structure of any chord will create another chord. This is why the term secondary arpeggio is sometimes used to describe this technique.

Shown below are the secondary arpeggios for the basic chords in a major ii-V-I progression.

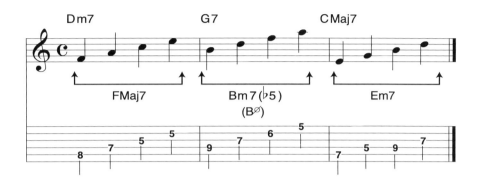

Playing the upper-structure of a chord is closely related to the technique of chord substitution that will be covered in a later chapter.

Targeting

Targeting has to do with approaching chord tones by scale tone or chromatically. There are a number of ways to target a chord tone. The first is by ascending and descending chromatic approach. This technique is shown below. It is important to realize that while the examples shown below use the chord tones from a C major chord, this technique may be used over any type of chord (minor, dim, etc.). (Notice the notes are arranged so the chord tones are played on the downbeats.)

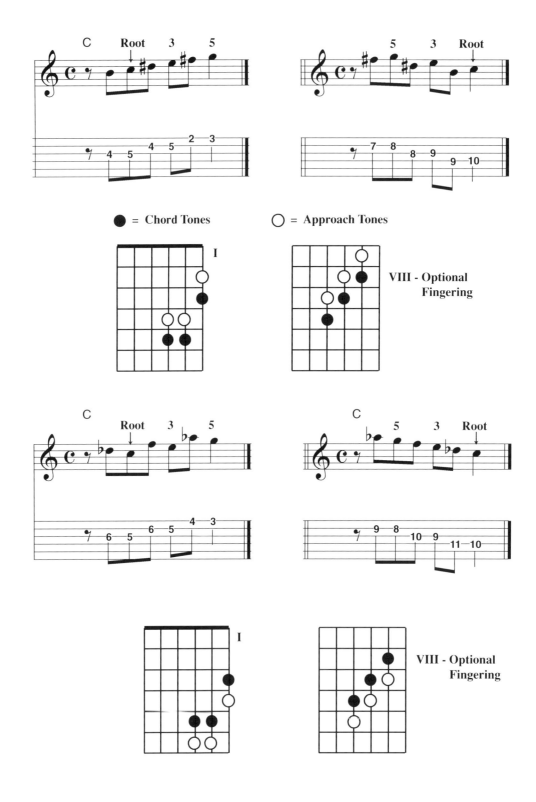

The next type of targeting is to use what many call an "enclosure." An enclosure uses either scale tones above and below or chromatic tones above and below to literally enclose a chord tone. For each of the sequences of notes discussed, the order of non-chord tones may be reversed.

The first type of enclosure makes use of a scale tone above and a chromatic tone below.

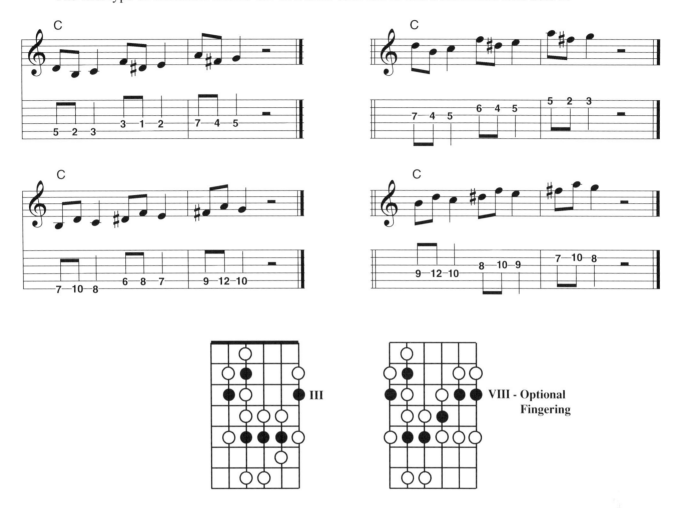

The next type of enclosure uses a scale tone below and a chromatic tone above.

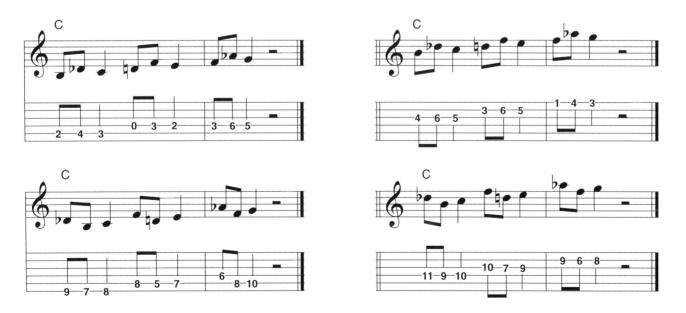

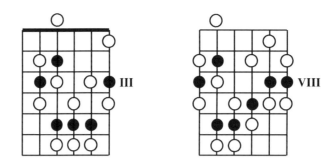

Three note enclosures combine scale tones above and below as well as chromatic tones above and below. A few examples of how this would apply to the root of a C major chord are shown below. Use this concept with all the other chord tones.

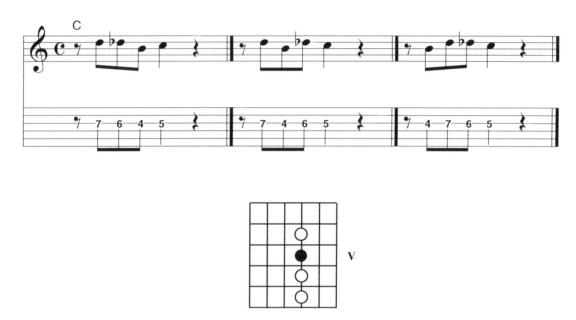

By combining scale tones and chromatic tones to enclose a chord tone, almost limitless possibilities of improvised lines may be constructed. Experiment with these combinations to create original lines.

The following line demonstrates how one might use the technique of targeting.

Arpeggios

The word arpeggio means "broken chord." An arpeggio is created when the notes of a chord are played in succession (ascending or descending in pitch) rather than simultaneously. Wes Montgomery made wide use of arpeggios in his solos. Having learned the music of Charlie Christian and Charlie Parker, he understood the importance of arpeggios in improvised music.

The following charts show the intervallic makeup (by scale degree) of major, minor diminished and augmented triads.

Major	Minor	Diminished	Augmented
1 (root), 3, 5	1 (root), ♭3, 5	1 (root), ♭3, ♭5	1 (root), 3, ♯5

This chart shows the intervallic makeup of major seventh (Maj7), dominant seventh (7), minor seventh (m7), half-diminished (∅7 or m7♭5), and fully diminished seventh (°7) chords.

Maj7	7	m7	∅7/m7♭5	*°7
1, 3, 5, 7	1, 3, 5, ♭7	1, ♭3, 5, ♭7	1, ♭3, ♭5, ♭7	1, ♭3, ♭5, ♭♭7

*The fully diminished seventh chord is made up entirely of minor third intervals. A minor third interval up from the flat fifth of a chord yields a double-flatted seventh scale degree. Students should note the half-diminished chord differs from the fully diminished in that it only has a flatted seventh degree. It differs from the minor seventh chord in that it has a flatted fifth. (Thus the other title of m7♭5.)

The example below shows the chords found in a C major scale. In every major key the I, IV, and V chords are major triads, the ii, iii, and vi are minor triads and the vii chord is a diminished triad. When four note (seventh) chords are built from a major scale, the I and IV chord are major seventh (Maj7) chords, the V chord is a dominant seventh (7), the ii, iii, and vi chords are minor seventh (m7) and the vii chord is a half-diminished or minor seventh flat five (∅7 or m7♭5).

C Scale

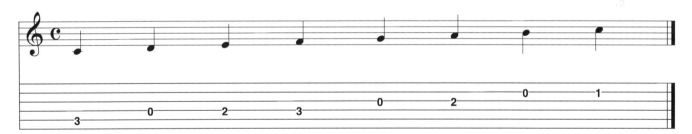

Triads in the Key of C

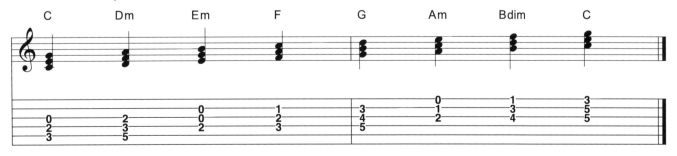

17

Four-Note Chords in the Key of C

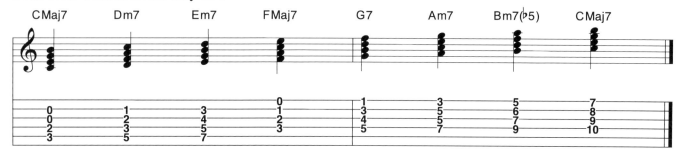

The following exercises will help players become proficient at playing and understanding arpeggios. For the "Wes" sound, play the exercises in this book attacking the strings with the right-hand thumb.

Ex. 1

Ex. 2

Ex. 3

Ex. 4

Ex. 5

*Each of the arpeggio patterns should be practiced in all twelve keys utilizing every area of the fretboard. Try mixing and matching the various arpeggio patterns. Alternate between ascending and descending patterns. Students should practice these exercises clockwise around the circle of fourths found below.

*Students may practice these arpeggio exercises with tracks #10 and #11 of the accompanying play-along CD.

*A portion of arpeggio exercise #1 has been transposed to all twelve keys following the circle of fourths. Use this example to transpose each exercise in its entirety..

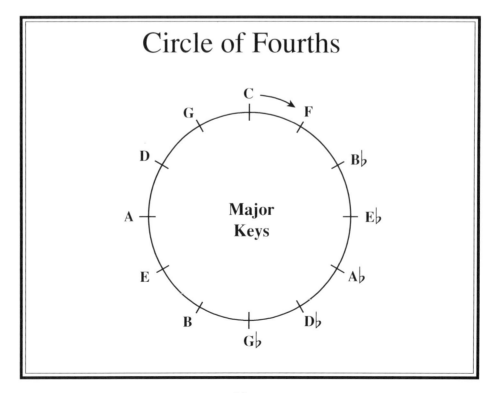

Transposed Arpeggio Examples

Playing Octaves

One of the most innovative and unique aspects of Wes Montgomery's playing was his use of octaves in single-note solos. Wes used octaves to thicken up his sound and give warmth and depth to his lines. By using the octave technique, Wes was able to give relatively simply melodies a unique sound. Even a simple diatonic melody sounded fresh when Wes played it with octaves. Fingerings for octaves (played on every other string) are shown below.

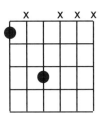 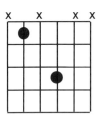 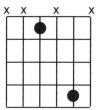 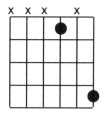

To master the technique of playing octaves, many scalar and arpeggiated exercises using octaves have been provided below. The exercises have been written in the keys of G and C. These types of exercises should be played in all twelve keys. By playing the exercises in two different keys, guitarists will be able to move the exercises to the other keys. The fingerings provided by the tab are only suggestions. Guitarists should experiment with their own fingerings and find the most comfortable positions for them to play these octave exercises. To get an authentic "Wes" sound, guitarists must attack the strings with the right-hand thumb.

G Major Scale

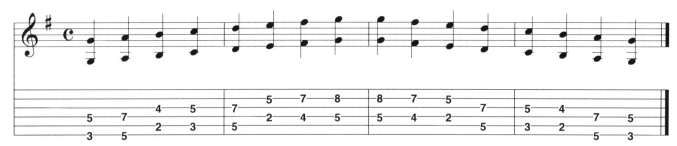

Ex. 1

Ex. 2

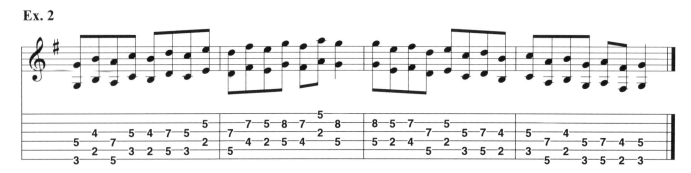

Ex. 3

Ex. 4

C Major Scale

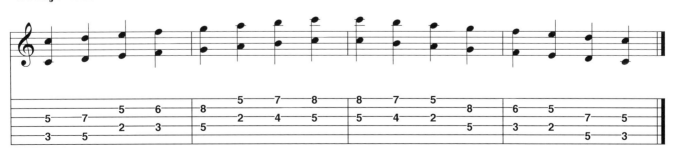

Ex. 5

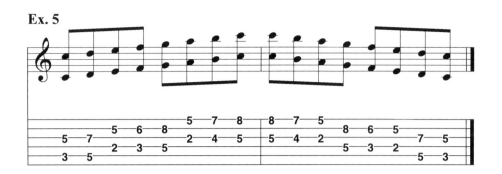

Ex. 6

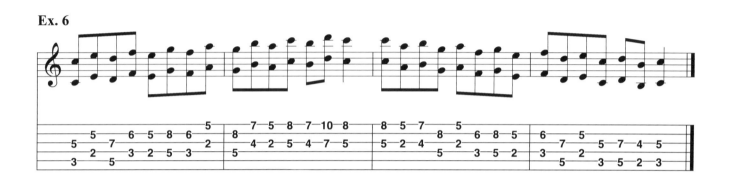

Ex. 7

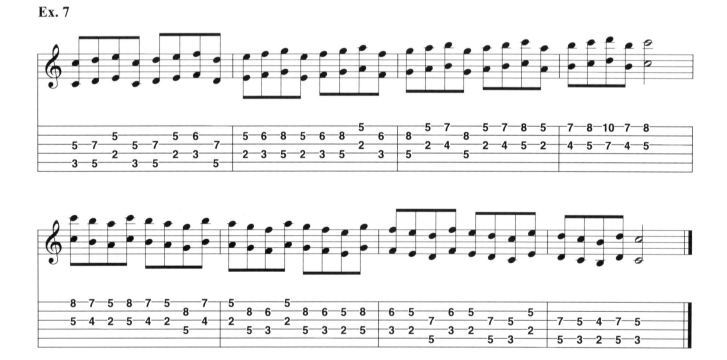

Ex. 8

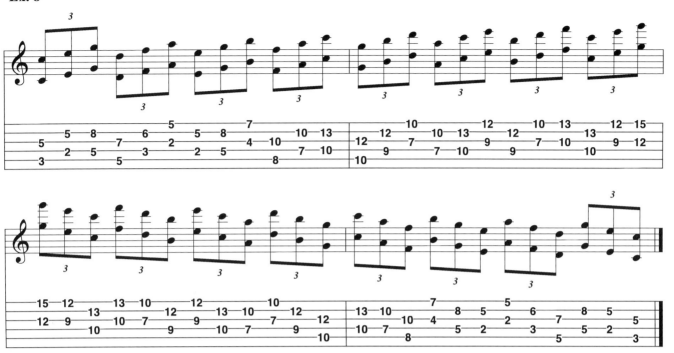

Guitarists may find that it is challenging to alternate notes played with octaves between strings five and three and strings four and two. By practicing these exercises well, any guitarist will be able to play octaves anywhere on the guitar.

Ex. 9

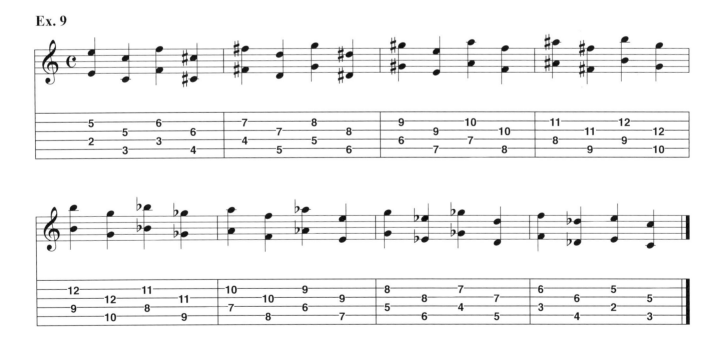

Ex. 10

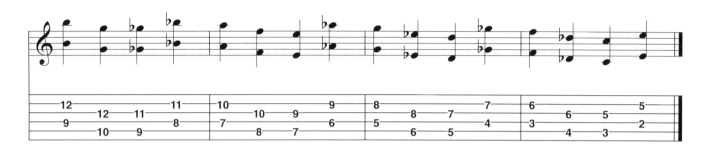

Here is a typical jazz line over the ii-V-I progression in the key of C.

Here is the same line played with octaves. Notice how the line takes on a "Wes Montgomery" type of sound.

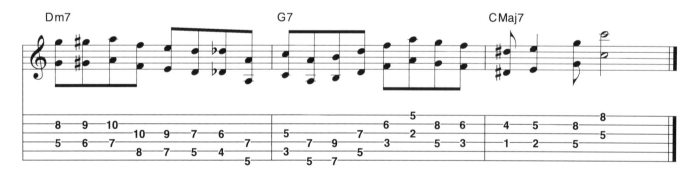

Experiment playing jazz lines with octaves. Wes used octaves to create a musical effect. Guitarists who want to incorporate Wes's sound into their own playing need to be proficient at playing lines using octaves. Experiment playing the single-note lines in this book with octaves.

Block Chords

Wes Montgomery frequently used chords on the first four strings and chords played on the inside four strings (strings two, three, four, and five). Like most jazz guitarists, Wes used these chord voicings when comping. Wes would also use these chords in his improvisations. Wes mastered the art of chordal improvisation on guitar. By using a plethora of chord shapes, Wes was able to harmonize many single line phrases with a four-note chord. Wes would often begin his solo with single-note lines, build the solo's intensity by moving to octaves and then bring the solo to a climax with block chords. The following diagrams show some of the chords that Wes frequently used when improvising. Be sure to master these shapes in all twelve keys.

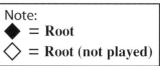

Note:
◆ = **Root**
◇ = **Root (not played)**

Major Seventh
(Maj7)

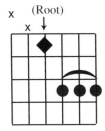 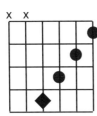 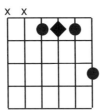 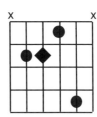 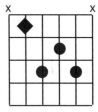

Minor Seventh
(m7)

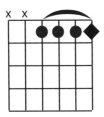 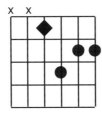 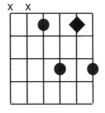 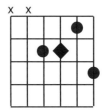

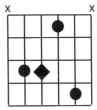 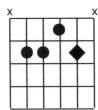 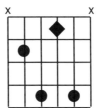 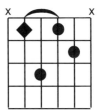

27

Minor Seventh Flat Five/Half Diminished
(m7♭5, ø7)

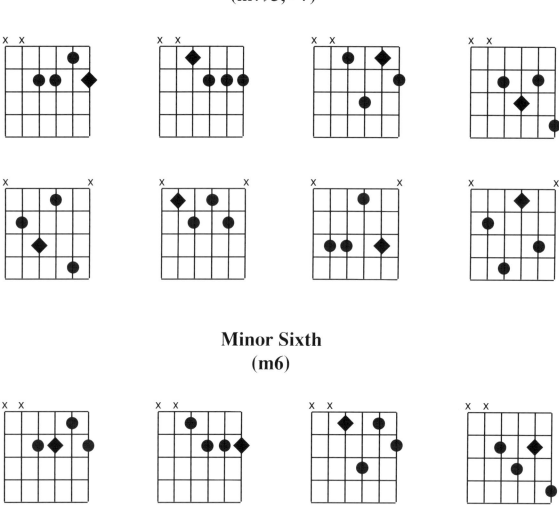

Minor Sixth
(m6)

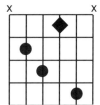 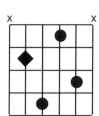 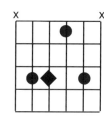 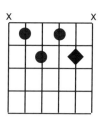

Minor Nine
(m9)

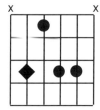 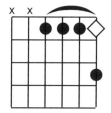

Minor Eleven
(m11)

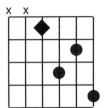 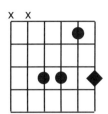 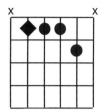

Seventh
(7)

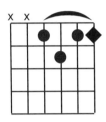 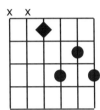 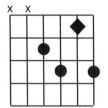 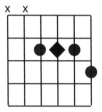

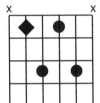 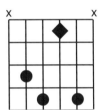 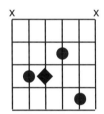 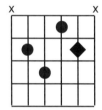

Seventh Flat Five
(7♭5)
(These chords have two notes that can be the root.)

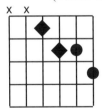 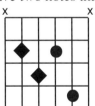 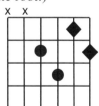

Seventh Sharp Five
(7♯5)

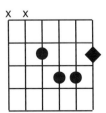 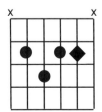

Seventh Flat Nine
(7♭9)

*In these two 7♭9 chords, the ♭9 replaces the root of a dominant seventh chord which creates a diminished seventh chord. Therefore, there are four assumed root notes for these voicings.

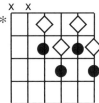 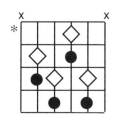 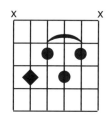

Seventh Sharp Nine
(7♯9)

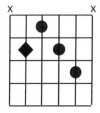 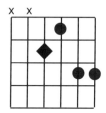

Seventh Flat Five Flat Nine
(7♭5♭9)

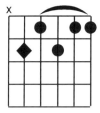 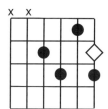

Seventh Flat Five Sharp Nine
(7♭5♯9)

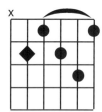

Seventh Sharp Five Flat Nine
(7♯5♭9)

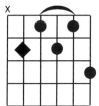 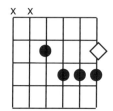

Seventh Sharp Five Sharp Nine
(7♯5♯9)

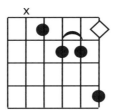 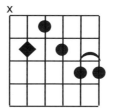

Ninth
(9)

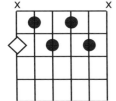 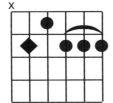 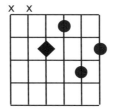 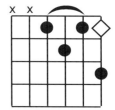

Eleventh
(11)

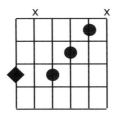 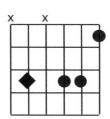

Thirteenth
(13)

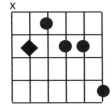 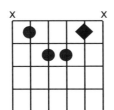 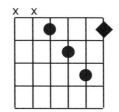 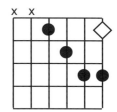

Diminished Seventh
(O7)

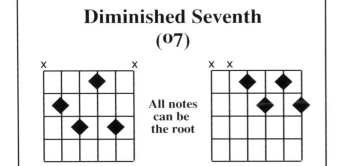

All notes
can be
the root

Augmented Seventh
(aug, +)

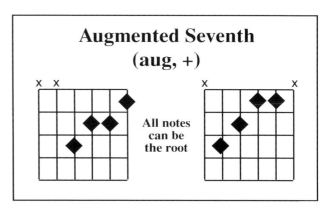

All notes
can be
the root

The following example shows how Wes could use four-note chords to harmonize a scalar line.

Notice these examples make use of a few chord substitutions to harmonize the line more effectively. For example, a B♭Maj7 and C7 is used while harmonizing the G Dorian line. Techniques of chord substitution are covered in the next chapter.

Chord Substitutions

Wes Montgomery was a master of chord substitutions. This chapter will introduce some common chord substitutions that Wes used in his comping, improvisations, and compositions.

The ii for V Substitution

The first substitution is the ii for V. Wes frequently played ii chord material against the V chord and visa versa. The chart below shows the ii and V chords in all twelve keys. Because the ii chord and the V chord come from the same major scale (Dm7 and G7 come from the C major scale), they share the same scale tones. For example, the D Dorian mode and G Mixolydian scale are made up of the exact same tones. By using chord substitutions, Wes was able to emphasize different tones in the scale giving his solos a modern and sophisticated sound. The following examples show how Wes would use chord substitutions in his soloing. Wes also used this technique in his comping. Students should experiment with this chord substitution when comping. Remember that the ii chord may be used in place of the V chord as well as the V chord may substitute for the ii chord. This technique works well in modal ii chord and V chord tunes where the harmonic background is stagnant.

Key	ii Chord	V Chord
C	Dm7	G7
*C♯/D♭	D♯m7/E♭m7	G♯7/A♭7
D	Em7	A7
E♭	Fm7	B♭7
E	F♯m7	B7
F	Gm7	C7
F♯/G♭	G♯m7/A♭m7	C♯7/D♭7
G	Am7	D7
A♭	B♭m7	E♭7
A	Bm7	E7
B♭	Cm7	F7
B	C♯m7	F♯7

*Enharmonic notes are two notes that have the same pitch but different name. An example of this is C♯ and D♭. Two chord names have been provided for the most common enharmonic notes.

Chord Scales

C Major

33

D Dorian (ii Chord Scale)

G Mixolydian (V Chord Scale)

D Dorian Lines (play with CD track 4)

G Mixolydian Lines (play with CD track 2)

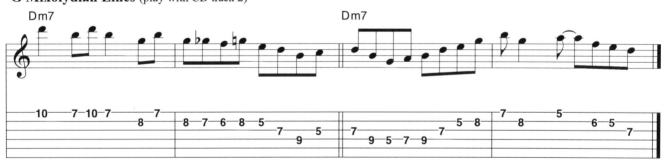

The ♭V for V Substitution
(Tritone Substitution)

The next substitution is the ♭V for V substitution. When a dominant seventh chord is being played, a dominant chord a tritone away (interval of a flat fifth) may be played. A chart showing the tritones for all twelve keys is shown below.

V Chord	♭V (Tritone) Substitution
G7	D♭7
G♯7/A♭7	D7
A7	E♭7
A♯7/B♭7	E7
B7	F7
C7	G♭7
C♯7/D♭7	G7
D7	A♭7
D♯7/E♭7	A7
E7	B♭7
F7	B7
F♯7/G♭7	C7

When a dominant seventh chord has a flat fifth degree, it becomes the enharmonic equivalent of a dominant seventh chord with a flat fifth degree a tritone away. Understanding this concept will help musicians see why the ♭V for V substitution can work so nicely when comping, improvising and composing.

The following examples show how to improvise using the ♭V for V substitution.

Ex. 3 (play with CD track 8)

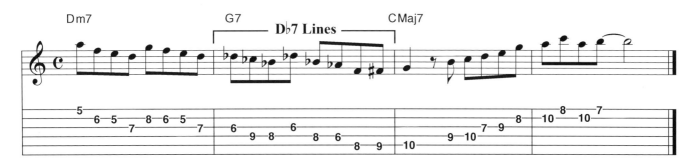

Ex. 4

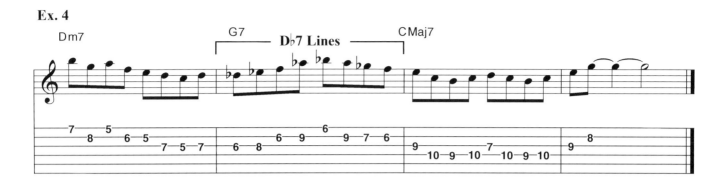

To add even more tension to the ii-V-I progression, Wes would occasionally add a ♭V substitution for the entire ii-V section. When this substitution is applied to a four-measure ii-V-I progression in the key of C (Dm7-G7-C), the chords played are Dm7-G7-A♭m7-D♭7-C. In this example, the ii for V (V for ii) substitution is also used to create more harmonic motion. Practice this substitution for ii-V-I progressions in all twelve keys.

Ex. 5

Ex. 6

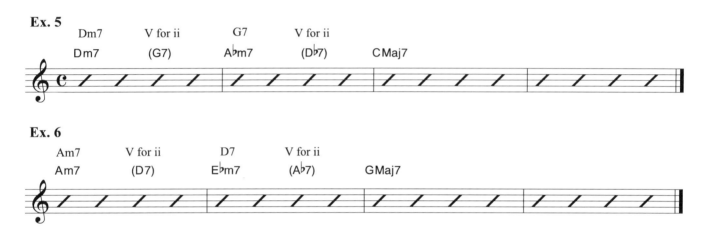

Wes also made use of other diatonic chord substitutions. Diatonic chords are the chords that belong to a parent scale such as the major scale. The chords in a major scale and their related modes are shown below.

I Chord	ii Chord	iii Chord	IV Chord	V Chord	vi Chord	vii Chord
Maj7	m7	m7	Maj7	7 (dom7)	m7	m7♭5
Ionian Maj. Scale	Dorian	Phrygian	Lydian	Mixolydian	Aeolian Nat. Minor	Locrian

By using a diatonic substitutions, Wes could think of and play lines that would work over a B♭Maj7 chord while a Gm7 chord was being played (relative minor or vi for I substitution in the key of B♭). If a D7 chord was being played (V chord in the key of G major), Wes may have played lines that would work for a Cmaj7 chord (the IV chord in the key of G). Even though diatonic chords are derived from the same key and therefore have the same notes in their modes (chord scales), by thinking and playing around a diatonic substitution, a less predictable, interesting and sophisticated sound is created.

Students should familiarize themselves with every chord type in all twelve keys and be able to substitute any of the diatonic modes when improvising.

Solo Development

Developing a solo was one of Wes Montgomery's greatest strengths. One of the reasons his solos were so melodic (his solos, at times, sounded "compositional" rather than improvisational) is because he could work with and develop a musical idea melodicly or rhythmicly. Because of the length of this book, a complete analysis of these techniques can not be covered. It is hoped that this chapter will shed light on developing melodic and rhythmic ideas enough to help students understand the way Wes played and help them create better solos themselves.

A basic type of melodic development is created by sequencing scales (scalar patterns). Many scalar sequences have been presented already to assist in the learning of arpeggios and playing octaves. Being able to sequence scalar ideas is the first step to sequencing melodic ideas.

To create original scalar patterns (sequences), simply assign each of the notes in the scale a number. The chart below shows assigned numbers for each of the notes in a major scale with the root on the sixth string. Next, a numerical pattern is formulated. Start out with a simple pattern such as: 1234, 2345, 3456, and so on until all the assigned notes are used. Simply play the notes in the order of the pattern. Practice formulating many scalar patterns. It is suggested that the pattern groupings stay between two and four notes.

Remember: each sequence may be reversed by playing the numerical sequence backwards.

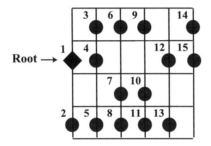

Sample Numerical Sequences:

1-2-3, 2-3-4, 3-4-5, 4-5-6, etc.

1-3, 2-4, 3-5, 4-6, 5-7, etc.

1-2-3-1, 2-3-4-2, 3-4-5-3, etc.

Ex. 1

1-2-3 2-3-4 3-4-5 etc...

Ex. 2

1 - 3   2 - 4   3 - 5   4 - 6   etc...

Ex. 3

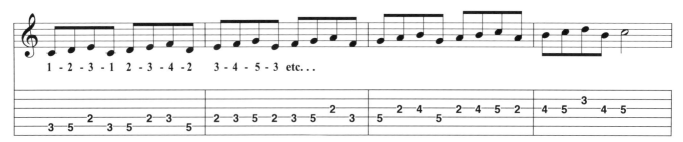

1 - 2 - 3 - 1   2 - 3 - 4 - 2   3 - 4 - 5 - 3   etc...

Remember: Each sequence can be reversed by reversing the order of the numerical sequence.

Sequence 3 reversed

8 - 7 - 6 - 8   7 - 6 - 5 - 7   6 - 5 - 4 - 6   etc...

A "Wes type" scalar pattern:

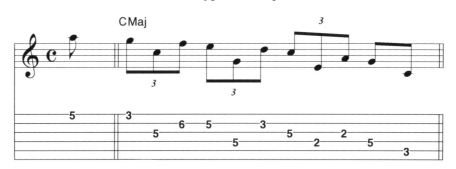

Modulation and transposition is another way to develop a solo. Wes was a master at moving musical ideas into new keys (G major to C major) and/or changing a musical idea's tonality (major to minor). Examples of both of these are shown below. Select tracks from the accompanying play-along CD will help students to modulate ideas around the circle of fourths. It would also be wise to first practice any major tonality ideas with the major chord play-along and then manipulate the ideas to work with the minor chord play-along. Hint: To change a major idea into Dorian mode idea, simply flat the third and seventh degrees of the scale. To change a major idea to a natural minor idea simply flat the third, sixth, and seventh degrees of the scale. To change the major idea to a harmonic minor idea, flat the third and sixth degrees of the scale. To change a major idea to a melodic minor idea, simply flat the third degree of the scale only. Examples of transposition and modulation can be seen on the following page.

To transpose ideas into another key, figure out each notes relationship to the tonal center, assign it a scale degree (1-7), and move to the new key. Be sure to make note of chromatic tones (sharped and flatted notes).

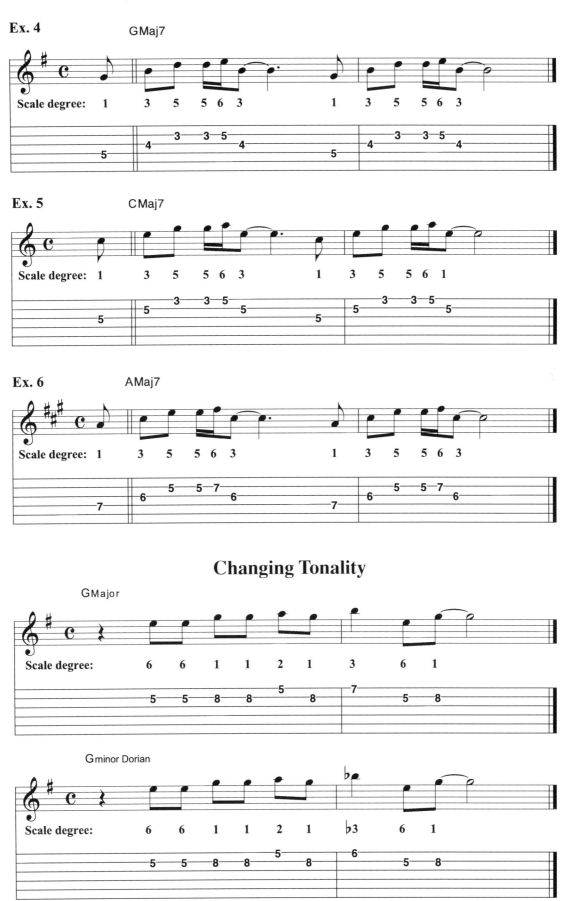

Changing Tonality

Another way to develop an idea is to embellish a motive or musical idea. To embellish means to ornament or beautify. The examples below show how a simple line can be embellished for melodic development.

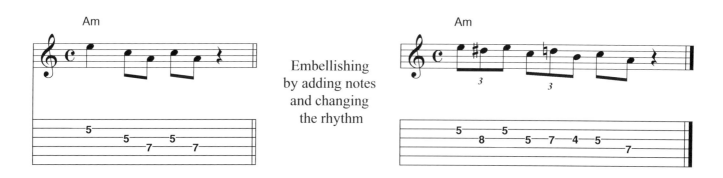

Embellishing by adding notes and changing the rhythm

Embellishing by adding notes and increasing the number of beats

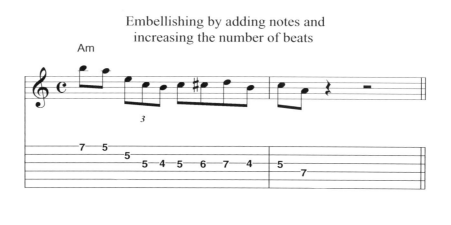

40

For this section, the student must select a line to master, practice it in the given key with the accompanying play-along CD and then use the CD track that modulates in fourths to master the line in all twelve keys. By combining minor chord lines with dominant seventh chord material, musicians will be able to mix and match numerous combinations of these lines to play over the major and minor ii-V-I progressions. Because the major and minor ii-V-I progressions are common in jazz tunes, it is crucial that students of jazz improvisation are fluent in soloing over this progression in all twelve keys.

Minor Ideas

The following lines may be played over minor seventh chords.

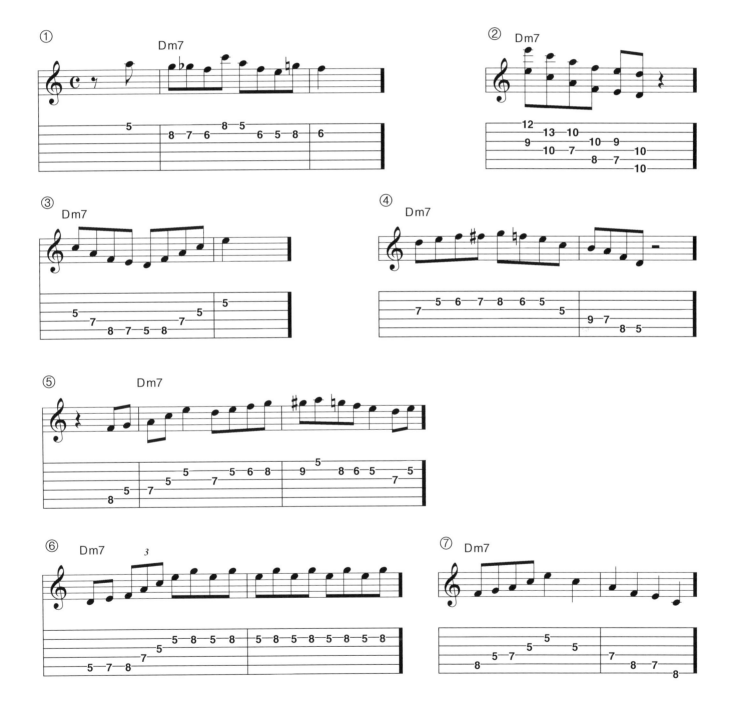

Minor Chord Vamp

CD #2

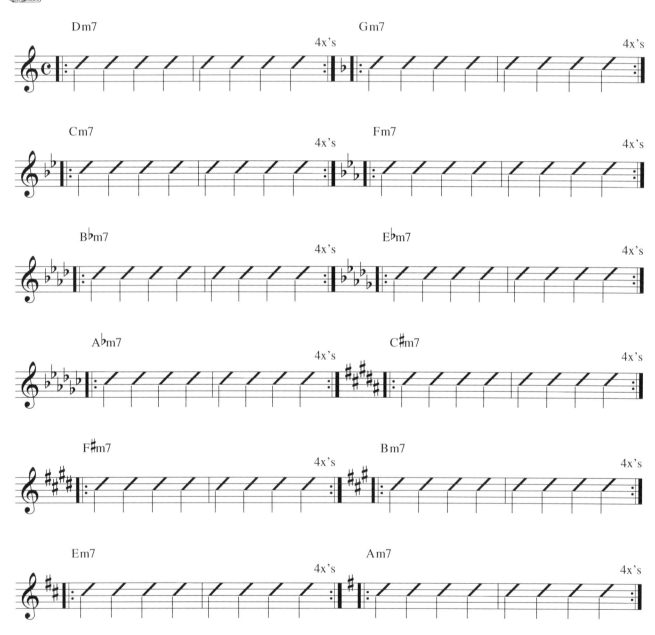

Minor Moving In Fourths

CD #3

44

Dominant Seventh Ideas

The following lines may be played over dominant seventh chords.

45

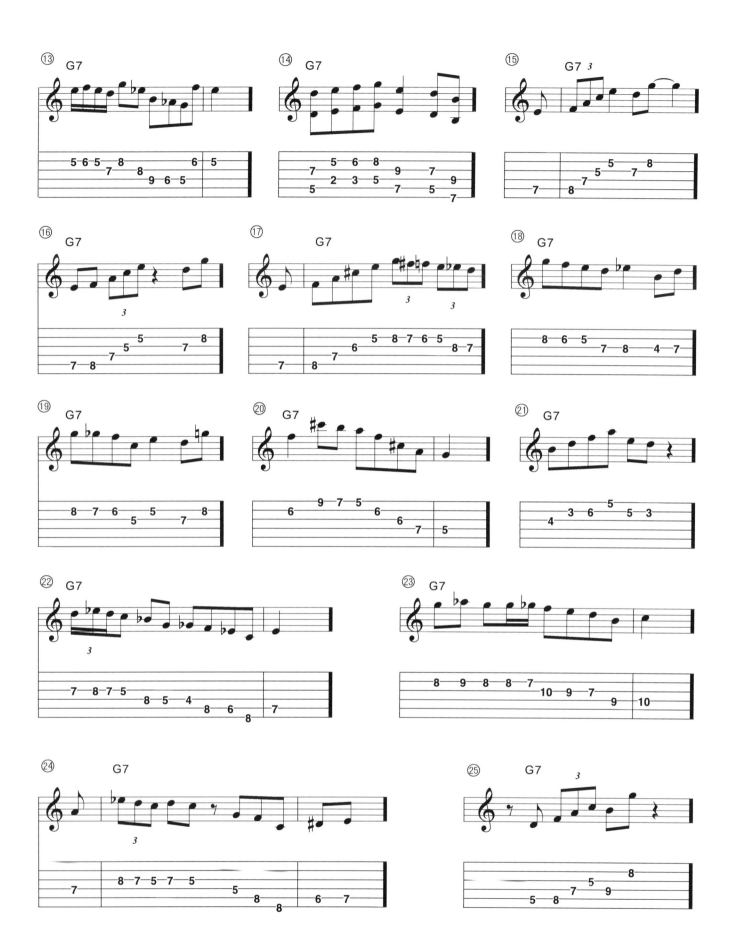

Dominant Seventh Vamp

Dominant Seventh Moving In Fourths

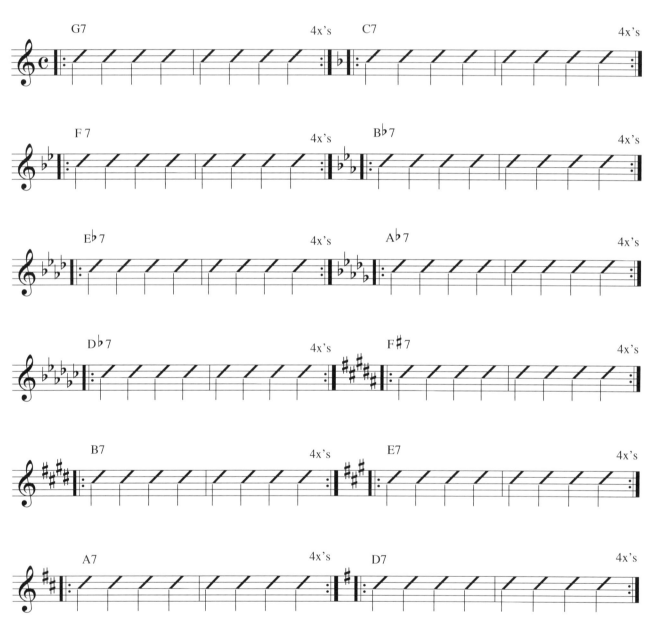

Short ii-V Ideas

The following lines may be played over short (one measure) ii-V chord progressions.

Short ii-V Vamp

Short ii-V Moving In Fourths

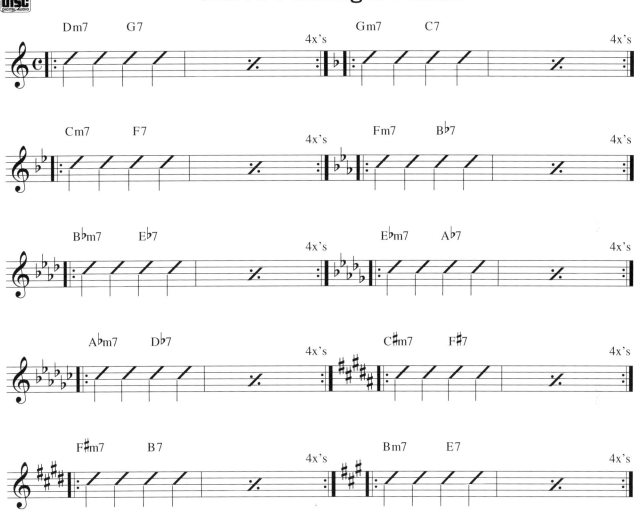

Long ii-V Ideas

The following lines may be played over long (two measure) ii-V chord progressions.

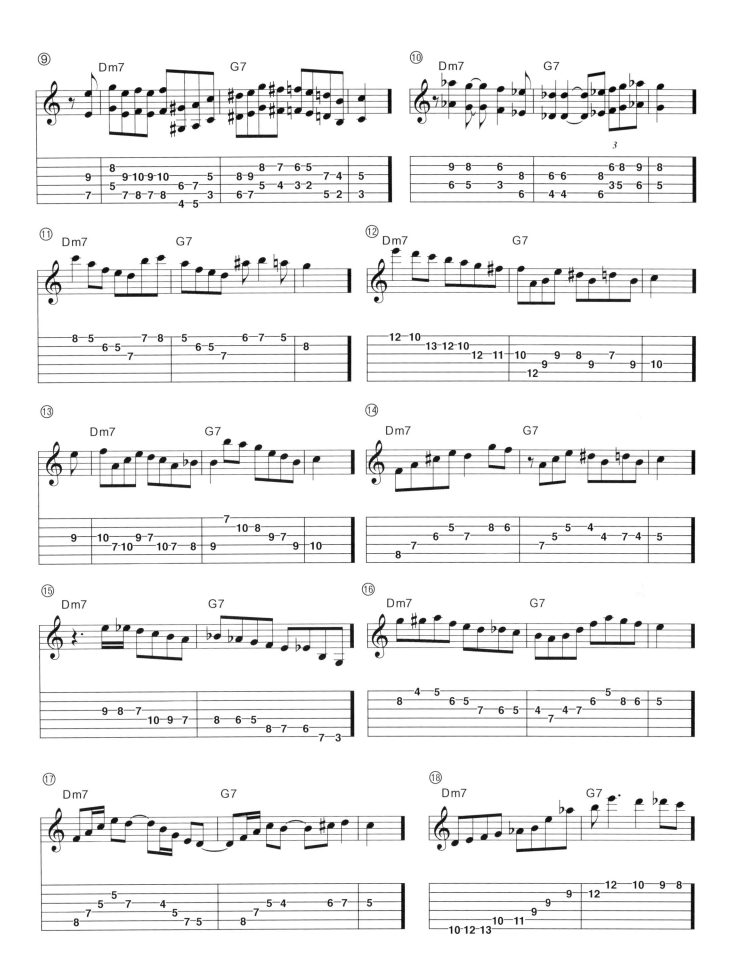

Long ii-V Vamp

Long ii-V Moving In Fourths

Major Ideas

The following lines may be played over major chords.

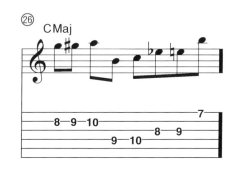

Major Vamp

 CD #10

Major Moving In Fourths

 CD #11

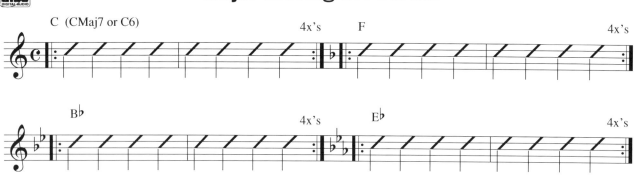

58

Minor ii-V Ideas

The following lines may be played over short (one measure) minor ii-V chord progressions. These lines will resolve to a D minor chord.

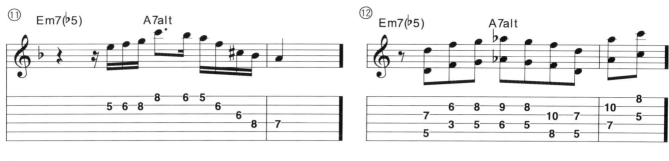

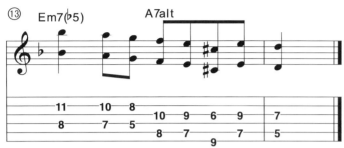

Minor ii-V Vamp

CD #12

CD #13

Minor ii-V Moving In Fourths

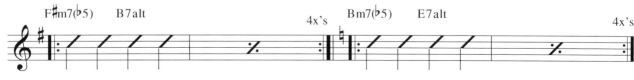

By combining ii, V, and I chord material, any musician can play eloquently over the ii-V-I progression. The following rhythm tracks have been provided so the student can practice combining material to play over major and minor ii-V-I progressions.

Short ii-V-I Vamp

Short ii-V-I Moving in Fourths

Long ii-V-I Vamp

CD #16

Long ii-V-I Moving in Fourths

CD #17

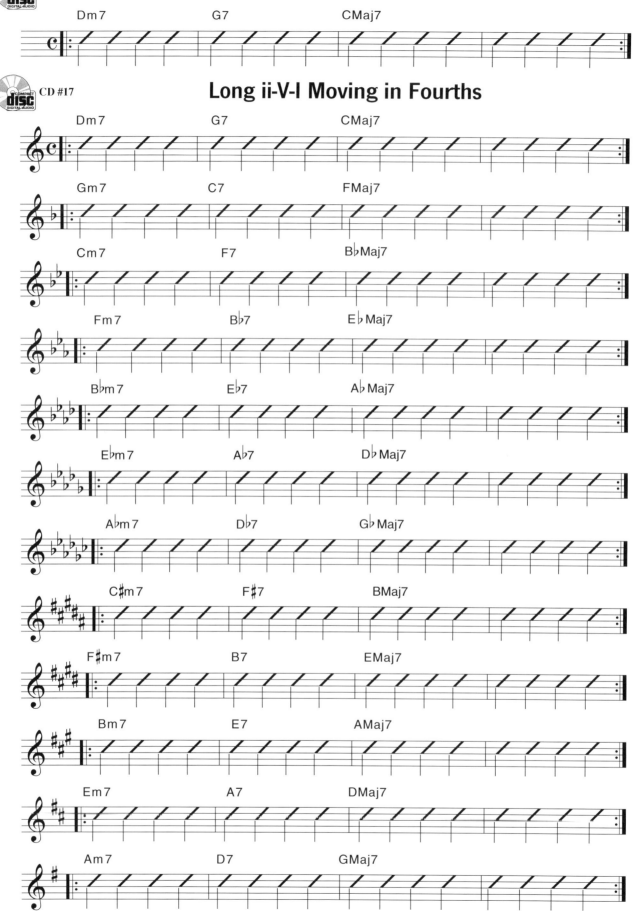

Minor ii-V-i Vamp

CD #18

Em7(♭5)   A7alt   Dm7

Minor ii-V-i Moving in Fourths

CD #19

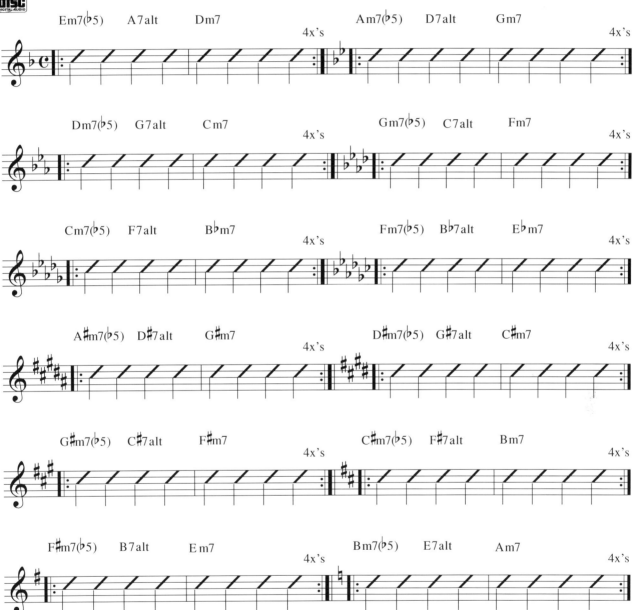

Em7(♭5)   A7alt   Dm7   4x's   Am7(♭5)   D7alt   Gm7   4x's

Dm7(♭5)   G7alt   Cm7   4x's   Gm7(♭5)   C7alt   Fm7   4x's

Cm7(♭5)   F7alt   B♭m7   4x's   Fm7(♭5)   B♭7alt   E♭m7   4x's

A♯m7(♭5)   D♯7alt   G♯m7   4x's   D♯m7(♭5)   G♯7alt   C♯m7   4x's

G♯m7(♭5)   C♯7alt   F♯m7   4x's   C♯m7(♭5)   F♯7alt   Bm7   4x's

F♯m7(♭5)   B7alt   Em7   4x's   Bm7(♭5)   E7alt   Am7   4x's

63

Turnarounds

A common turnaround in jazz consists of a minor ii-V leading to a major ii-V. The major ii-V resolves to the tonic major chord. The turnaround occurs two measures before the progression resolves to the tonic I chord. Because many tunes start with the tonic, the turnaround is commonly found in the last two measures of a tune. The chords Em7b5, A7alt, Dm7, and G7 make up a turnaround in the key of C. This progression is shown below. By combining lines that work over a minor ii-V progression with major ii-V lines, one can easily construct lines that work well over a turnaround. The examples shown below illustrate how to combine minor and major ii-V lines to improvise over a turnaround.

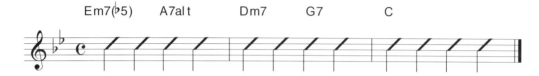

Example:

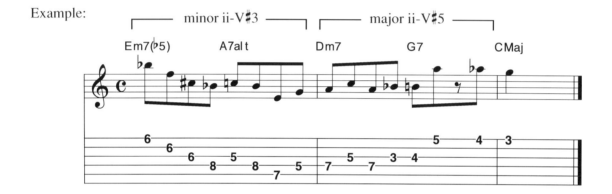

Turnaround Vamp

CD #20

CD #21

Turnaround Moving In Fourths

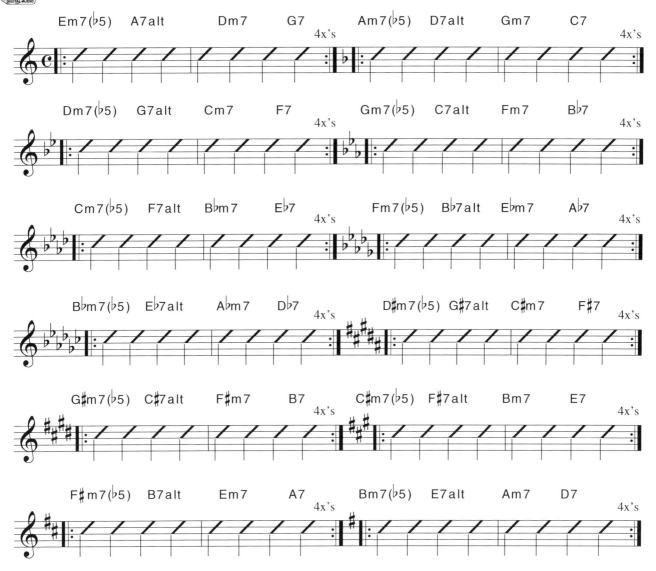

65

The following etude has been written to demonstrate how the lines presented in this book can be transposed and organized to create "improvised" solos. By mastering the ideas and concepts presented in this book in all twelve keys, guitarists will increase their ability to solo over most jazz standards and increase their improvising vocabulary. At times, the lines may be changed or manipulated to work with preceding or postceding lines.

Etude

The following play-along recordings have been provided to practice connecting the melodic ideas presented in this book. Also practice original material learned by studying the concepts and ideas from the beginning of the book (arpeggios, octaves, chord substitutions, etc.)

Progression Similar to "Misty"

Bb 12-Bar Blues

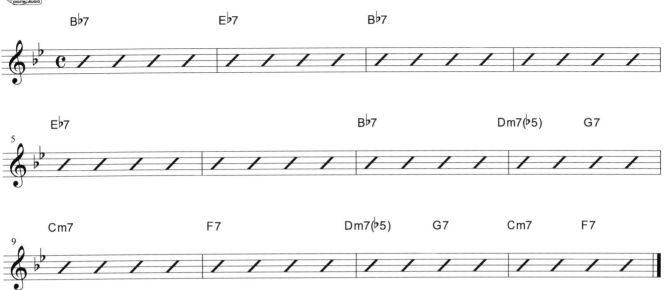